Conquering Trauma

D1827063

Why You Cannot Experience Peace And Joy And How To Finally Point Your Life In The Right Direction

By

Michael Vitela

Table of Contents

Introduction.............................. 5

Chapter 1: Comprehending Trauma..... 9

Subchapter 1: Visible And Invisible Types 9

Subchapter 2: Trauma As An Analogy 15

Subchapter 3: Trauma Defined 20

Subchapter 4: Trauma Responses....................... 28

Subchapter 5: Trauma Bonding 34

Subchapter 6: The Problem Of The Traumatic

Memory 41

Chapter 2: The Etiology Of Trauma.... 44

Subchapter 1: The Mind And Body Disconnection

.... 45

Subchapter 2: Patterns Of Trauma 47

Chapter 3: Practical Tools To Heal

Trauma 53

Subchapter 1: Levels Of Trauma 54

Subchapter 2: Meditation & Yoga 55

Subchapter 3: EMDR & Brainspotting................ 59

Subchapter 4: Counseling 62

Subchapter 5: Exercise 64

Subchapter 6: Grounding Exercises 66

Chapter 4: Understanding Recovery From Trauma 68

Subchapter 1: Healing Trauma 68

Subchapter 2: Coming Into The Present Moment 71

Subchapter 3 Factors & Variables Of Trauma 74

Subchapter 4: Trauma Disorders 79

Chapter 5: Learning To Heal 82

Subchapter 1: Paths To Recovery 86

Subchapter 2: Creating Structure 90

Subchapter 3: Self-Care 92

Chapter 6: The Silver Lining Of Trauma 96

Subchapter 1: How To Develop A Support Network 97

Subchapter 2: Learning To See & Embrace Our "Selves" 101

Chapter 7: The Stages Of Forgiveness

....**104**

Subchapter 1: Stage 1 Of Forgiveness.................107

Subchapter 2: Stage 2 Of Forgiveness................109

Subchapter 3: Stage 3 Of Forgiveness.................111

Subchapter 4: Stage 4 Of Forgiveness................ 113

Subchapter 5: Stage 5 Of Forgiveness................ 114

Conclusion **115**

References **119**

Disclaimer............................**124**

Introduction

Understanding trauma and its effects on your life is like trying to tie your shoes in the dark. Or perhaps, it is like trying to drive when there is a dense, opaque coat of fog encompassing you. Healing from trauma is not a leisurely stroll through the park. Figuratively speaking, I had to sludge through the mud, jump through rings of fire, and swim across large bodies of water to get to where I am today. Healing from one's traumatic experiences is undoubtedly difficult, but it is worthwhile in the end. It takes a commitment of time and an investment in yourself to move through this process of healing from your past.

This book entails an understanding of trauma through a couple of different lenses. The reason being is to learn about and conceptualize trauma in a way that is the most helpful to understand it. The first lens displays an understanding through analogy. The analogy allows for those who visualize ideas through metaphors and emotions to be capable of self-analysis by the end of the book. By learning to access the primitive part of your brain, you'll be able to recognize the emotions pertaining to your experience. This newfound knowledge will help you to feel seen, heard, and known when it comes to learning how to heal from trauma.

The second perspective explains trauma through definition and identifies what trauma is and what it is not. I will describe patterns of trauma and how it is often generalized. Understanding patterns of trauma will help shed light on our part in keeping the wound with us. I will depict variables and evidence of the impact trauma causes to a person both mentally and psychologically. I will also share stories of individuals who suffered from trauma but eventually succeeded in the battle to understand it or overcome it. All this will help you identify your trauma and realize the power you have to defeat it.

There are several ways in which one can address their

negative life experiences. The premise is that the healing and growth are all within reach; we have the answers in our minds and bodies. The parts we have control over are how we deal with and work through our issues or adversities. You will learn what daily self-help tools are and how to find and use them, which will aid you in your journey to heal.

I learned to liberate my mind and body through some intense work in self-care and to listen to my body. I found that healing the mind comes faster and easier than it does in the body. Of course, this is not always the case, but I want to emphasize that understanding methods of healing can help you reclaim the power that you've forgotten, and ultimately lost.

Overall, the purpose of this book is to help you recognize trauma in yourself and others. The knowledge gained through this book will provide an understanding of individuals and their responses to adverse life events. The answer is not to enforce what other people have utilized that works for them, but to get in touch with yourself again and gather what you need. So, take what serves you and let go of what does not. It is merely up to you to choose how you want your life to look from here forth. Dig deep and uncover what is holding you back so you can live a life of freedom. You are worthy of every second of a shameless, grace-filled, joyous-centered life, free of the cumbersome burden of trauma.

Chapter 1: Comprehending Trauma

If you suffer from the lasting effects of trauma, you may feel as though you have no control over your emotions and thoughts. Because of the engulfing feelings associated with your negative experiences, you may even feel powerless to creating change. The first step to overcoming trauma is to identify thoughts and behaviors that stem from negative experiences of your past. Once you can identify negative thought repetitions and overpowering emotions, you can trace your way back to the root of the issues at hand. Let us look at the different types, responses, and definitions to establish a base and starting point.

Subchapter 1: Visible And Invisible Types

There are visible forms of trauma that have an evident impact on a person, but there are also invisible forms of trauma that are masked from the world and buried deep in the heart. When you see someone acting aggressively or withdrawn, they may be reacting from a place of fear and tribulation. The individual is not likely acting out without reason; they have been hurt before, and you are in the crossfire of their emotional unhealthiness. You must understand the difference between what thoughts, emotions, and actions are your responsibility and what is theirs.[6]

The obstacles that prevent us from moving out of this place are our fears. Fear is the center of our thought processes when one is functioning from past experiences. I will provide more information on the brain on trauma throughout this book to glean comprehension of what is going on neurologically. The anxious cognitions likely echo the following: they will reject me; they might not like my opinion, I will be abandoned and alone, or they could hurt me. These thoughts can easily take on a snowball effect and escalate into more feelings of anxiety and worry. Then, ultimately, the cycle continues where we choose to react to the situation accordingly so that we can prevent any possible pain. We use this method to protect and keep the invisible wounds from worsening.

However, this cycle is a paradox because what we think will protect us does the opposite, and often leads us to what we worry about most.

The invisible wounds can be dreadful and excruciating or may even appear to be non-healable. When considering early childhood, you may recall a memory where you were bullied in the 3rd-grade on the playground or harassed by an older sibling. There may even be memories of abuse occurring throughout the house in which you grew up. If any of your thoughts come from a negative belief you have of yourself, or a grim emotion, these may be signs of your invisible wounds. Without any treatment of these wounds, you continue to feel a stinging sensation when you encounter a similar interaction. Later, you may come across a similar experience that felt like rubbing alcohol was being poured over the injury, and the agonizing throbbing does not cease. Suffering lingers when you do not examine what initially caused your struggle. Each incident of the same or similar issue occurring builds on the untreated trauma and deteriorates how we think, feel, and what we believe to be true about ourselves.

Additionally, emotions and actions stemming from traumatic events may build on the original hurt and reoccur. For example, a person may ascertain to treat themselves and others in the way they were initially hurt. Emotional disturbances that are long-suffering become what a person knows to be the reality. If a mother yelled or scrutinized them countless times, it is not unheard of if this person goes on to treat others in this manner.

There is a dance to how visible and invisible wounds intertwine and keep you stuck and sick. When I continually try to build walls up between others and myself, I do so as a form of self-preservation against the hurt I fear will incur. However, my external behaviors do not lead me to what I need to heal, and instead, continue to isolate me. I begin feeling more discouraged and trapped within my own fear and wallow in defeat. Subsequently, depression increases and hopelessness takes up a larger space within me. This mindset may direct me to ill coping methods, such as substance abuse or self-sabotaging behaviors that affirm my negative emotions. Thus, the cycle continues as it is focused on the response of the person to an event and how that can intensify, worsening the reactions altogether.[10]

Fortunately, while trauma repetition can ensue a cycle, there is a spot where you can intervene and stop the pattern.[10] One of the most difficult tasks of remediating these adversities is to step out and change what is hindering you. Naturally, your mind and body may feel turned upside down and find change to be uncertain or unattainable. This transitional period is an important time to speak kindly to yourself and welcome the unknown, as what may have kept you alive before is not helping anymore. After you become aware of the impact trauma has had on you, you befit the responsibility for keeping the cycle of trauma from continuing. You were not responsible for the actions of the individual(s) who harmed you, but you have the accountability of stopping yourself from spreading that hurt to another. It is crucial to identify the cycle to distinguish your role and your power in determining whether it continues or ends.

The first action you can take on exiting the repetition of trauma is to explore what your visible wounds are. Essentially, these are the unhealthy actions or language you use toward yourself or others. More examples of these behaviors may be restricting nutrients to punish yourself or serial dating the same belittling and uncontrollably angry type of person. Once you can see what is not abetting you to do well, you can start working on changing those behaviors. I like to think of it as cutting off the dead stems that keep you from growing new, more efficient characteristics. I've listed helpful tools later in this book to unearth the positive, healthy traits and behaviors you hide beneath negative emotions. Once you discover those invisible wounds are dictating your actions and words, the change will not be as foreign or petrifying; it will become enticing. This affirmative action will take you on a path to cleaning out those seemingly bottomless invisible wounds, chopping off the dead branches, and beginning the healing process.

Subchapter 2: Trauma As An Analogy

At the bottom of the ocean lies a life unknown to most: a land unseen. It's almost as if the floor is a hidden treasure or a mystery, yearning to be discovered. This unknown land is a lot like trauma, it is stored deep within you, and it is seeping out in one way or the other. It is only a matter of you taking the time to invest in your healing to let it take you under or to float serenely.

The sea brings the mind to focus and awakens you to how expansive the world is and how finite us humans are. It is delicate and playful, all while being subtly violent. The waves appear to be cradling you as you rest upon them, then, roaring toward the shore and pummeling the sand. Then, there is a tranquil moment of the water cascading up the coast, toward the beach shore and receding to meet the darker water again. There is a gentle grace and intimate connection between the land and the sea when that happens. It is as if the ocean is displaying our humanity and how we are all connected. We are brought together by the summation of our experiences, the intense memories, and the universality of emotion. Each of us has our own stories and our pasts, but we are not alone in this battle to overcome our worst moments. We get to swim through this ocean with others if only we look around to see that more bodies are trying to stay afloat with us, or generously handing us a life jacket.

When considering this analogy, the shore appears to be relatively serene on the outside, and it is hard to envision anything wrong. This facade is the front we put up to most people with whom we interact. The thought is that as long as they can see us smiling and managing our lives, the stronger and more acceptably pleasing we are. However, a little deeper in and the waves are crashing and wreaking havoc on the shoreline. The waves represent a person's unhealthy behaviors, negative thoughts, and dark emotions to what is going on beyond the shore. This chaos is what is truly stirring behind that mask of perfection. The rest of the ocean represents the abyss of distressing memories; it is everything that fuels these dark and negative feelings or actions. Still, the shore helps us to disguise the internal anguish and to keep our "oceans" hidden because if others knew the truth, we might feel vulnerability and shame overwhelmingly. Any time I suppress an emotion, I regress the ground I am making towards recovery. Thus, I am not allowing myself to heal or manage the emotion. Instead, I am bidding to grasp at control in any way I can, to prevent that feeling from arising again. This withholding of dreadful feelings will, in turn, creates an unhealthy thought process, behavior, and lifestyle for me.

The inherent nature of trauma is stifled with shame; it teaches us that we are alone in the pain that we experience as a result of the experience. There is much to be said about the emotional response to trauma. A person who experiences trauma may react differently than another with a similar traumatic experience. For instance, if two people experience abuse from their caregivers, one may internalize the fear associated with the abuse, and cannot function well in society. The second person, however, may not hold onto the trauma because it does not disturb them psychologically.

We will discuss a few examples of how this may play out. Person 1 was physically abused and neglected by his parents at an early age in childhood until the initiation of his adolescence. How would you imagine him to be coping with this experience? I would guess that he does not understand how to cope with the confusion and uncertainty brought upon him by his parents. They were not present the majority of the time, but when they were, they were physically aggressive toward him. In his best attempt to understand the love that he expected his parents to give, he begins to associate physical aggression as love.

After all, by acting aggressively, he received the most attention in his childhood. Depending on the age at which the trauma occurred, this will impact a person developmentally. They may learn they cannot trust any authority figure or that they should avoid intimacy, as it will only result in abandonment. Growing up, he does not learn any differently. He continues this "loving" way by imposing aggression upon others for whom he cares because again, he does not know any other approach. This is what is hidden underneath the surface of his "waves."

Likewise, Person 2, who had the same circumstances and relational dynamics with his parents, was able to respond well or work through that issue and does not carry that burden with him. There are several factors that could have changed the consequences for Person 2. He may have had other caregivers who provided him with healthy attachment and met his needs. He may have gotten to receive counseling and other support to work through his trauma. An impactful way to handle trauma is to reparent yourself and connect with your inner child. There is no shame in not having what you needed as a child. This ties into the control you have overtaking your life back and living it without those anchors of defeat.

Subchapter 3: Trauma Defined

To take you a bit further, here is the premise of what trauma is and what it is not. Trauma is the emotional response to an event, such as sexual assault, natural disaster, or combat. There is a long list of events that may lead a person to become distraught and/or harmed. Commonly, when someone goes through a life-altering time, their mind aids them by setting up a means of defense. These defenses can be dissociation, which is when a person has an out-of-body experience that results in repressed emotions associated with this event. Concurrently, when that person encounters a trigger, the response may be to shut down or disconnect. The fear response exemplifies the lengths the mind goes to shield you from harm. [i]

The midbrain houses the fear center, where reactions like fight, flight, or freeze reside. These are the three main reactions to danger. Let us use a classic example of the well-known relation to the disorder, Post-Traumatic Stress Disorder, or PTSD. For instance, someone from ground combat in the military, who endured gunfire every which direction, has learned to respond to this noise by fighting back or flying from the battleground. This person's brain will recall the piercing echoes from the war as soon as they hear a broken muffler on a car or ignited fireworks. The brain does not only recognize the loud sounds as a possible danger while at war, but thereafter. A person can quickly revert to the emotion associated with the previous trauma. This reaction is known as having a trauma response, and ultimately not rationalizing with the logical part of the brain to know one is safe and the original event does not presently exist. It is crucial to find a solid object or a healthy, trustworthy person to latch onto for support. This symptom of PTSD is called a flashback, which presents a replay of the disconcerting event, which can be reopened by the senses. Another standard sensory response is when one smells a familiar scent that they associate with a traumatic incident. For example, if an individual was assaulted or mugged by a person wearing cologne or smelt strongly of tobacco, they may have a fearful response upon identifying the same scents. We will delve into more of the specifics of trauma responses later on.

One dynamic variable of a negative reaction is the length and complexity with which one can endure. Exposure, whether direct or indirect, can also impede one's daily functioning. I learned early on in life some untrue statements were instilled in me when I was mistreated. These negative words included: "I am not good enough", "I am dirty", "I am unwanted." It turned out that these thoughts, paired with the shame and fear circulated through my mind, made me hypervigilant of anything that would similarly represent these untruths. Then, I found myself drawn to circumstances that would feed the undesirable monologue in my mind, deepening my shame and fear.

In this instance, I had worsened my suffering by subjecting myself to further instances that kept me down and reinforced my negative emotions towards myself.

Additionally, my issues were further multiplied by the secondary trauma of being a counselor. As a counselor, I must be mindful when helping my clients with their own traumas, as it may bring up some of my own. It is healthy for me to be able to utilize my story to empathize with and support others; however, this can yield detrimental effects, too. If I were overly involved in a client's life, it would not be helpful for either of us. The same goes for overidentifying with their personal history and lacking emotional boundaries. A healthy relationship is one of balance between supporting my client and pushing them to find better outlets of dealing with their dark emotions. This dynamic does not just appear in a counselor-client relationship; it may be present in other relationships with friends, family, spouses, or coworkers.

Just remember, you are not alone in this battle to reclaim yourself. There are many people, if not everyone, who will go through a life-altering event at one time or another, and they too will embark on finding themselves again. Trauma works as a façade for the inherent traits a person exhibits; in the healing process, that façade begins to fade, and your authentic self begins to arise. Anyone who has suffered in the past can reclaim control over their lives with a bit of guidance and support. There are numerous avenues to find healing from hurtful experiences, and we will reconnoiter many of them so you can identify the best routes to take. Of course, choose the recommendations that fit for you and what you may need at the given time. This may even shift as you proceed through your trauma.

The brain is influentially cunning and powerful, able to react quickly based on emotional responses. It is noteworthy to understand what happens in your mind when a potential threat or harm triggers you. Because of these fear response types, trauma can be defined as the mind-body-soul shockwave resulting from a negatively life-altering event. Again, think natural disasters, homelessness, abuse, neglect, loss, domestic violence, war, or divorce.

These categories of trauma are the catastrophic occurrences or heart-wrenching pain that are considered "big T" traumas. These traumas are classified as major life events that cause a significant change to a person's world after the event. Consider the impact these types of events may have on yourself; I am guessing there would be feelings of terror, shock, or dismay. Due to the fear-evoking nature of these incidents, a person's reaction to them is where the brain becomes deregulated and altered. Since trauma is the response a person has, as opposed to the event, you can see that there is a significant correlation due to the emotional impact it instills. [ii]

The "little t" traumas are instances such as an argument with a loved one, being reprimanded by an authority figure, or falling off a bike. I believe the majority of us experience a multitude of "little t" traumas throughout our lifespans. We may not register them as traumas, but our bodies and minds take note of these as episodes to be avoided in the future. The little "t" traumas do not outwardly create a life-change, but they do accumulate over time, which is where the "filing system" of the mind comes into the picture. The filing system has a history of each time you experienced a state of trauma. Often, it affects our self-beliefs, schema of the world, and personal values. Most traumas are not self-flagellating; they are typically the reception of another's hurtful action that is the cause. The pertinent part of this is we have the power over how we respond to it. That is the piece of the puzzle that keeps us bound to our past.

Trauma repetition adds to the complexity of the trauma as the individual reenacts a traumatic event that occurred. For instance, if a woman had an emotionally neglectful father, she will likely seek out romantic relationships with men who treat her similarly as a subconscious attempt to resolve childhood issues and to seek out normalized relationships. The mind believes that if we can find the same person with a different haircut, we can innovate a solution. It is common for a person to relive their trauma based on the emotional and mental state they were in when they experienced the initial event. Another example is if a person who is being abused lies still while feeling helpless as abuse is occurring, seemingly frozen in place. There is a likelihood that a caregiver, coach, or teacher performs the abuse; someone trusted and in care for the child. A child, then, may believe early on that abuse is a form of love, and it becomes what they find consolation in. In turn, this consolation may cause trauma repetition as they continue to cycle onto those they love in the future.

Chaos becomes second nature. It is what is known and understood – this comfort refrains an individual from changing, as anything different is unknown. If there is any boredom, idle time, mundane activity, or feelings of apathy, one will presumably seek out the uncontrollable manners of disarray to get high from adrenaline and familiarity in what is known. When one has comfort, familiarity and a sense of belonging, they will likely head that direction and avoid the path not yet walked. More so, an individual who has learned to accept the damage as "normal" may not be able to identify a need for change or may have a fear of change. Take these considerations into the next subchapter, as we will break down the responses.

Subchapter 4: Trauma Responses

Consider a time when you felt that tightness in your chest and your palms sweating. Anxiety rose within you, and you noticed your logic silence itself, and emotions take the lead. Your reaction is due to the type of fear response one has, which falls into the categories of fight, flight, or freezes. A trauma response can vary, depending on the duration of exposure and the severity of the trauma. For instance, when an individual responds by freezing, there is no way for the tension to be released and it may produce a more severe impact on the brain. That individual's mental unhealthiness may increase over a length of time if the freeze response becomes a more common reaction. The primary reason for this is because a person will endure worse violence or pain, as they cannot find the wherewithal to fight back or flee. The reaction to a traumatic event is the trauma; it is not the actual occurrence itself. Whether that is abuse, neglect, war, or any other trauma, it is how the person's body and mind fathom it.

Aforementioned, the fight, flight, or freeze responses are the brain's biological acknowledgments of turmoil. There is an additional response, called fawn, which is a less familiar and more common response. We discussed the first three responses and discussed the reaction to the stimulus at hand. There are many more situations that you may have witnessed or experienced; an example is seeing a car crash down the street that may cause you to emotionally react if you withstood a car crash in the recent past. Reason will inform you that you are safe and there is nothing happening to you, but the memory of your experience will return. Experiences affect how an individual responds to an event and can influence a response by recalling the emotions felt within that event. The frontal lobes are responsible for higher functioning, that is reasoning, decision-making, morality, values and logic; however, fear clouds the ability to reason. Basically, higher functioning goes out the window, and the response to the potential threat is taken on by the fear center. The fawn response is when a person inhabits people-pleasing, impressionable and codependent traits. [7] This response is typically caused by intense feelings of rejection, and the victim will likely attempt to succumb to the ways of their perpetrator or care for others more than themselves.

Moreover, when a person's brain cannot handle the trauma stimulus, they go into the deer-in-headlights mode and freeze. The freeze response is one in which a person is fearful, but cannot direct the panic effectively, and thus becomes numb to the peril. An everyday illustration of this is when a person is riding a roller coaster; their fear center takes the reigns and sees that there is not much control over the 50-foot vertical drop. A person can only sit in their seat and wait for the ride to end, too petrified of the drop to even scream. All fear responses are intended to be functional and protective, yet some may have the opposite effect.

A fear response is not healthy if it becomes a non-effective method of self-preservation. The "freeze" state, for instance, can worsen the level to which the brain is impacted and the extension of time it takes to rewire it back to its "normal". In an instance where a person recognizes the peril as overpowering and ultimately, undefeatable, the body and mind go offline and protect danger from infiltrating. You may have heard that when people freeze in response to trauma, it may not be as appealing to the attacker as if you were to fight back. It is common for children to have this response, and it may be helpful in certain situations. However, when the freeze response occurs in adulthood, it is nowhere nearly as beneficial. What was adaptive as a child, dissociating from an event vastly beyond your capacity to handle, can become frustratingly maladaptive as an adult. Yet, in adulthood, our prefrontal cortexes are fully developed around age 26, and as a result, we have access to more coping skills. When we have coping skills, then the trauma response is no longer needed, and we can deal with the situations that arise with a healthy approach.[4]

Moreover, there are levels of hyperarousal and hypoarousal that a person experiences as a result of trauma triggers. This is the window in which a person retorts to a certain situation with a level of tolerance to their anxiety. The identifying factors of hyperarousal are feeling flighty, ungrounded, riled up, or unhinged. This is most closely related to the "fight" response, one where you feel the impulsive urge to act violently toward yourself or another. If one is experiencing hypoarousal, this looks more like being unaware of reality, being catatonic, or feeling apathetic. Your system wants to shut down may look more like a flight, freeze or fawn response. Thus, the grounding tools we will discuss are some options you can practice when you are feeling an emotional disturbance or experiencing triggers. ⁱⁱⁱ

Characteristically, when an individual responds to a potential threat by way of fleeing, they will continue to flee situations that appear similar to the initial trauma. The same applies to other responses to fear. Generally, you will hear that a person who has served in the military may have PTSD as a result of the traumatic events they witnessed or experienced. Perhaps when they are taking a stroll outside and hear a loud motor, their amygdala switches into gear, and this person responds by way of their go-to fear response. The goal of trauma work and healing is to help an individual connect their limbic system to their prefrontal cortex without the associated fear response to the triggering stimulus. When this occurs, a person will respond to that stimulus without the emotional disturbance initially paired with the traumatic event. They will simply notice the event, and recalled their own experience, but will be able to manage their reaction.

We will discuss treatment for this in later chapters.

Subchapter 5: Trauma Bonding

There is a peculiar relational dynamic that occurs between two or more people; the concept is known as trauma bonding. This transpires when two or more people experience an undesirable event together and are bonded because of it. People can correspondingly emulate trauma bonding when they have not gone through the adversity together but have had similar situations or emotions, and thus relate to each other. In these situations, there is an immediate connection with that person; it makes you feel understood and safe. Often, the people in this type of bond understand their relationship to be very close and intimate. It is important to have bonds with others and support through difficulties, but bonding over negative experiences has the potential to depress and hinder you, at which point it is not a healthy style of attachment.

There are a few styles of attachment that are worth knowing about. You have access to assessments when you look online, as these will help you pinpoint which style is most like your own. The main styles of attachment are anxious, codependent, avoidant, disorganized, secure, and preoccupied.

- An anxious attachment style is one in which you lack trust due to fear of potential abandonment or rejection. The initial experience of relating to one's caregiver and their affection and attention toward you is strongly correlated to the attachment style you develop. In the case of anxious attachment, a child was likely to see their caregiver act in nervousness and be overly cautious about safety and wellness. This type of attachment style bleeds out into many relationships. One may not have much trust in their self, which amounts to them having self-doubt, low self-esteem, and feeling insecure. This style of attachment may result in codependency and the emotional reliance on the other person to support one's needs. The way the caretaker models meeting the child's needs in an anxious manner is closely observed and learned by the child. The child learns to handle many situations and relationships with this style of attachment.

- Codependency is the lack of emotional boundaries and self-confidence, seeking external validation. Codependency forms out of one's need for attachment, but not in the healthiest way. Paradoxically, one who identifies with this style will seek intimacy and relationship with another whose attachment style is predominantly avoidant. Those who exhibit these attachment styles are usually drawn together, but ultimately pair like oil and water. When one lacks an emotional boundary, they allow the feelings of others to affect them. Likewise, they do not have a filter to let in the good and keep out the bad. This person may believe that if the other person is okay, then they are okay. Often, they do not understand that they are not responsible for another person's emotions. A person may be acting in ways where they are exclusively reliant on a romantic partner or their adult child to be what they need and to meet their expectations. To get to a healthy style of attachment, one can develop a secure/healthy attachment style by learning from others who are secure. The most contradictory style is the avoidant attachment style, where a person usually disengages from potential intimacy with another.

- Avoidant attachment is where a person dodges emotional dependability and commitment. This style of attachment forms when a caregiver ignores a child's needs altogether. The child learns that he/she cannot rely on others to be reliable and meet their needs. Underneath this is a person who inherently wants to have the ability to be intimate with and commit to another person, yet their unhealthy attachment will hold them back. The reason I mentioned that anxious and avoidant attachment styles do not pair well together is that they cause a tug-of-war dynamic in their relationship. The anxious attachment style will seek out attention and affection from the avoidant, and the avoidant will run from this. Then, when the anxious person distances themselves a bit from the avoidant one, the avoidant one draws in further, where it feels safe, and they do not need to worry about attaching. Next, the anxious person feels relieved that the avoidant is closer to them now, and the avoidant retracts again. This also relates to the next attachment style, which describes this pattern of ambivalence.

- A disorganized attachment style is wishy-washy in the sense that a person identifying with this style may be comfortable being with another person one day, and the next, they feel so frightened by the closeness that they then try to avoid the other person. This is similar to the anxious and avoidant relationship dance, yet disorganized attachment can be complex by how indecisive a person would be with building a rapport and a bond. At times, they might find themselves to be preoccupied with the other party involved. It becomes disorganized, and until realized and treated, the person continues the cycle of dichotomous attachment.

- Preoccupied attachment is best described as a person who is constantly worried about receiving the approval of others, particularly with romantic relationships. The biggest fear, or at least one of them, is that he/she will be rejected and not loved as much as they love the other person(s). The mind is consumed by the external influence on this individual, and he/she thrives off of how well the relationship is doing. The problem here is that this person does not have that self-trust and internal motivation to thrive without another person there. This way of relating, along with the other styles of attachment, can be more predominant in certain relationships and appear healthy and secure in others.

- Secure attachment is the ultimate goal when it comes to the way we interact with and relate to one another. One can choose what values, beliefs, or opinions of others one wants to keep or ignore entirely. When you do this, you just let it go and keep moving forward, whereas before, in an unhealthy attachment style, you may have ruminated on this remark for hours, days, or years. When you become securely attached, you recognize your self-worth and respect yourself not to let a minute statement from another person destabilize you. It is not about being linked to another person, where you have stability in your relationship. This is on you to take ownership of what you need to work on to become the secure and confident person you are.

Looking at attachment styles on a deeper level and identifying the one with which you connect most is paramount to being able to find the core of your wounds. When discovering and working through traumas, one will see that their relationships with themselves and others have been impacted. Once you being this work, you can decide what you need for support and self-care.

Subchapter 6: The Problem Of The Traumatic Memory

Some people will say that it does not matter what happened, as it is in the past and does not affect you anymore. Unfortunately, that is the furthest statement from true when it comes to traumatic memory. Traumatic memory is when one remembers the memory of pain so strongly that they cannot move past it. Furthermore, when there is a traumatic memory, it is not only held in the brain in memory but becomes a continuous reality. Thus, the memory still feels alive and present with us. When this is the case, it is not possible to simply leave the past in the past.

Instead, the traumatic memory keeps the fear and pain in mind. This often comes out by way of impulsivity and acting in survival mode. Though the reality is that the damage and harm that was done is not occurring in the present day, the vividness of the memories makes it feel that way. Our brain registers it as such, too. This is even more of a reason to know that you are not crazy. You are not the insane cycle or set of behaviors in which you act out. It is the trauma that is steering the ship, and thankfully, we get to do something about it.

It is possible to remove the impulsive, out of control, flippant behaviors, and thoughts. It is possible to restore the mind and create a healthy way of living. This is where the goodness is cropped from the bad that once existed. Paying it forward and being able to help others to heal is another way to reclaim your power and control over your life.

Our trauma response can appear in many facets of our lives. A trauma response may consist of unhealthy coping mechanisms, cognitive distortions, addictions, suppression, regression, etc. It is innate for us to adopt patterns that reflect the trauma(s) we experienced earlier on in life. When a person experiences trauma for an extended period, they may start to enjoy or be comfortable with chaos or excitement. Eventually, this may even become addicting. This is largely due to the brain being rewired by the traumatic event or events. There are remnants of emotional discord that settle into our bodies post-incident.

Chapter 2: The Etiology Of Trauma

To fully understand trauma, it is pertinent to understand its origins. When something adverse occurred in the past, what gives it the notion to continue to exist in the present day? I want to review all that occurs to keep the trauma in motion. There is a disconnection or dissociation of the mind from the body. This may be more commonly known as an "out of body experience", where you envision yourself apart from your physical being. This is another instance in which some of the patterns formerly mentioned might have originated. Also, note the cyclical and layered disposition of trauma and how trying it is to progress through a new cycle of healing, instead of repeating. Regardless of the work, it is far more rewarding to be diligent and perseverant in overcoming each of these barriers, than it is to linger as a foundation for suffering.

Subchapter 1: The Mind And Body Disconnection

There is a resilient, palpable connection between the mind and body. There is some solid evidence through research that has been done to show the correlation and causation amongst the two. Or rather, I should say the dissociation that occurs as a method of protection and self-preservation, when exposed to the stimulus. If a person is continually exposed to trauma, the body shuts down and becomes disconnected from the reality of the hardship.

Additionally, by keeping the distress inside and not processing through it, the trauma will form into physical illnesses or diseases. We will look at a Caucasian, middle class, married, woman. She lives with her spouse and their two kids. Her presenting problem is Substance Use Disorder. She experienced a copious amount of health issues, leading her to abuse opiates and other narcotics. She stabilized and adjusted to admitting into treatment. When she was cleared medically after detox concluded. Then, the deeper work began. Thereafter, she began articulating her underlying issues. She revealed that her father had an affair early on in life. Subconsciously or unconsciously, this trauma stuck with her. A cycle of conceiving and miscarrying sent her down a spiral of her own extramarital affairs. She disclosed that she became "obsessed" with having a baby. She stated she would seek out men who were the same race and ethnicity as her spouse, so if/when she became pregnant, he would not suspect infidelity. This was the secret she buried so deep within her; she explained that she frankly forgot because it was so suppressed. As she continued her counseling work, she began to uncover a secret that she had buried deep inside of her. She never told her husband that their now 10-year-old daughter is not his biological child. She believed she had the right amount of support around her and the courage to disclose this to her spouse. The conversation with her spouse happened, and he expressed his anger about finding private email accounts and a random assortment of material items retrieved from these men. He became filled with pain and grief of finding out about these affairs, and worse yet, learning that his daughter was not biologically related to him. Ultimately, he agreed to work on their relationship. And, so, the cycle of trauma is reciprocated.

Subchapter 2: Patterns Of Trauma

There are a couple of patterns of trauma that are worth noting if you personally relate to them. Some of the patterns are generational traumas that are passed down the family line. Trauma is also cyclical; a person experiences a negative situation, then feels shame and hurt, and then replays the trauma by engaging in a similar relationship or situation. There are plenty of layers to the healing process. There are also different types of trauma: primary and secondary. Let us take a closer look at the patterns displayed in Person 1's case. This will identify the root and etiology of her trauma, health-related issues, and Substance Use Disorder. At the core of these issues, she began by way of her father's cheating. This is generational trauma.

Perhaps, his father or his father's father acted out this way, and he continued the cycle. She internalized this, whether knowingly or not, and it resulted in this profound manner in her own life. In this same vein was the shame and pain that continued to foster within her—and grew in secrecy.

Once she could identify this, she already felt relief and began to process further what this meant. Awareness is half the battle; the other half is accommodation. In life, one will come across memories, triggers, or situations that initiate a response recall, yielding a trauma response. This person may have a field trip back to childhood, and instantaneously undertake the same feeling she/he had when this experience first occurred. Often times, this comes later in the journey, and a person can be aware of the outside layer, which is the present and cumbersome circumstances in which they currently are. As the process of healing continues, the layers are shed, and one gets to the center of their trauma.

In actuality, this is likely to take a lifetime. Now, before this message gets misconstrued, I am not implying that one cannot heal from trauma. I'm suggesting that the layers of the past will continue to be shed as time moves along. If you understand yourself to be in the early stages of learning about trauma and recognize experiences of it in your own life, know that you will not always have the uncontrollable emotional responses to similar events. In 12-step meetings, there is a saying, "It works if you work it, so work it 'cause you're worth it". This applies to healing, too. Keep in mind that the time, energy, and money you put into your own healing is priceless when it comes to living a liberated and fulfilled life.

The concept of becoming friends with one's body to establish a connection between the body and mind is crucial. The "easy" route and the first one we will take is to attempt to shut out any and all pain we have experienced or currently endure. Anger, a secondary emotion, enters the scene as your sidekick, helping you to repress any "negative" emotion. Paradoxically, it is far more healing to welcome the presence of the mind-body connection. This is the crux of this paper—the part where to look at practical application and tools to use daily to begin or resume your restoration.

Primary and Secondary traumas affect people in differing ways. Enduring either event, whether directly or indirectly impacted, can yield similar negative effects. In consideration of the contracts between the two, I will inform you of the potentially life-altering effects that may result from either.

- Primary traumas occur when one is present at the scene of the event. This means either a person is the victim, or they have witnessed the incident. As an example, a child who witnessed domestic violence in their home will undoubtedly have anxiety, hypervigilance, and flashbacks. These symptoms can vary in severity and length of duration. Typically, this is based on the amount these issues occur and how intense they are. In the case where a parent is experiencing physical abuse by the other, the child will fear the perpetrator and take on the emotional unhealth from the victimized parent. This type of response can carry the child into being the parentified child. The way this happens is that the units of a family system will do what is necessary to try to balance the system of the family. When chaos erupts, like in this situation, the child sees that his/her caregivers lack in emotional, mental and psychological health. Thus, the child will work to bring this back to balance by taking responsibility for more than she should. Hence, why even a person who witnesses a traumatic event that is not directly inflicted, is primarily impacted by trauma.

- Secondary trauma occurs mostly for those who work with victims of a natural disaster, abuse, neglect, or other violence. These professionals may be firefighters, first responders, mental health professionals, or nurses in the ICU for a couple of examples. In my own experience, as a counselor, I can easily identify my own need for consistent self-care. I hear patients' stories of horrific and complex trauma daily. If I do not take appropriate measures to care for myself by getting massages, seeking counsel, sleeping well, eating healthy, and exercising, amongst various others, then I will burn out. Burnout occurs when a person is exposed to another person's traumatic history through stories and a relationship with this person. I believe humans are inherently connected and empathetic, and it is easy for us to take on other's pain if we are not careful to set and maintain boundaries.

Chapter 3: Practical Tools To Heal Trauma

There are plenty of ways to lighten the loads you carry when it comes to feeling weighed down from your grief. These tools are the core of changing an untrusted enemy (your body) into a valiant friend. Bearing in mind the spectrum of severity and complexity to trauma, you can see what is needed for treatment. Also, since not all levels of trauma treatment call for hospitalization, there are a plethora of other ways to go about recovering in the day-to-day. You can determine the level to which you need treatment, as well. A couple of habits I would suggest when taking this direction are meditation, yoga, counseling, integrative medicine, and exercise. What will become valuable to you is learning how to chaperon your thoughts and actions, too. If one of these methods feels more fitting for you, go with it. I do encourage you to try out all you can, to reconnoiter what may be helpful that you may not have been unaware of prior.

Subchapter 1: Levels Of Trauma

The levels of trauma differentiate based on exposure time, length of the occurrence, severity, and the symptoms. A level I trauma would need the highest level of care. If there is physical damage, a person would need to receive immediate medical attention and care. The need for stability and physical functioning is primary to the mental health aspects of treating trauma. There is 24-hour surveillance to ensure the client's bodily functions are operating within a normal range. This level is comparable to that of level II.

Level II requires a high level of care and management for a 24-hour period. The distinct difference is that these trauma centers do not have as many requirements as level I. Care for this level may have an arrangement of minor differences, too. Though this level is treated in a hospital, the injuries may pose less of a life risk.

Lastly, level III does not adhere to as many requirements as the first two levels do. One of the main differences is that level III does not call for in-hospital care. This is the most common level at which people are treated. A level III center may have patients who have broken their leg, or similar. At this level of treatment, a patient still has access to any medical treatment they may need, and the provider will arrive promptly to assist. [iv]

Trauma does not have to be mental; it can be how a person is physically impacted by an accident or fall. As stated, the trauma is the response to the person's experience. From a medical standpoint, the severity of the occurrence allows professionals to identify the level of trauma a person has imposed.

Subchapter 2: Meditation & Yoga

Meditation is a scientifically proven method aiding in the dissonance between the mind and the body.

Meditation allows for a person to grow in self-awareness of their thoughts, emotions, mind, body, spirituality, etc. The mind is the lens through which we experience the world, which is where our beliefs and values are. With this being said, it is pertinent to approach the rewiring of negative self-talk, to a more positive, self-loving approach. Another benefit of meditation is to be present with your emotions. Welcoming emotions in and accepting their coming and going, will be immensely helpful to you. Emotions are paper tigers; in the dark, they are frightening, but once you see them for what they are, it becomes clear that they are nothing of which to be afraid.

Yoga falls along the lines of meditation- it is a practice of aligning the mind and body. You may find yourself in a hot yoga class, in the downward dog position, for what feels like a lifetime, and it is there that you notice your strength and ability to persevere. Yoga is one of the best ways to reconnect the mind and body after experiencing dissociation during adverse experiences. When one is heightened by a negative stimulus, they may experience shortness of breath. Breathing is an efficient way to connect the logical and emotional parts of the brain. More oxygen flow to the brain helps reduce anxiety and tightness of the chest. To reiterate, the midbrain involves the amygdala and the hippocampus, which houses trauma and the fear center, and the Prefrontal Cortex is responsible for higher functioning, decision-making, and logic. Furthermore, the neurotransmitters within the neuron synapses decrease the "feel good" hormones so that the decision-making can occur.

Additionally, it is easier to be present and associated with reality in this state. I can think of many times I have practiced yoga, where I was in the awareness of my body, more than I had ever been. I am on this rectangular plastic mat for about 60-90 minutes. I do not go anywhere else; I just simply follow the teacher's guidance. I remember how rooted I felt. I was grounded in myself and recognized the true meaning of the relationship between the mind and body. It is here that I was able to let my thoughts and emotions come and go. I was not trying to control or change them; I humbly let them be there with me. It sounds easy, but trust me, I struggled and continue to struggle with this. It is challenging to let pain, fear, and anger be there in that small space with me. Yet, I am glad I do. Just like a paper tiger, it helped me learn that emotions are not large and petrifying. Emotions are nothing of which to be afraid.

On the yoga mat or in the meditative mind state, is an opportunistic place to reconvene with your inner child. Your inner child can be you at several different ages in your childhood, adolescence, and adulthood, depending on where you are in life. I will mention more about particular theories of counseling that assist in getting in tune with your younger selves. Your younger selves sometimes take the lead without having been properly parented and call for attention. You can notice this in yourself by thinking of a time where you felt you acted immaturely, pouted or went to a childlike place in response to another person or situation. You can start to see the parts of you that are yearning for care and love, by which ones prevail more often in an unhealthy way. By stilling yourself and contemplating on this, you can start to give yourself what you needed when you were younger.

Subchapter 3: EMDR & Brainspotting

Eye Movement Desensitization and Reprocessing therapy (EMDR) is one of the primary ways I have healed my mind. I mention EMDR, as it has been particularly useful to me in developing more skills than the survival ones I innately inherited and shed the layers of my past. This form of desensitization and reprocessing works by bilateral stimulation. Therapists are able to get certified for this, to be able to help clients' process through trauma at a faster rate. One way to look at it is to see it as EMDR accomplishes a lot in two sessions, while talk therapy is taking the estimated equivalent on eight sessions. This is like finding the key to unlock the vault of trauma and work through it to reduce the negative emotional association originally paired with the trauma.

Bring back to mind the different trauma responses one might portray. A brain on trauma can be stuck in the flight and freeze modes from a very early age. It is only natural that this brain continues to move in that direction any time there is an encounter of peril. Even if a potential peril is an empty threat, my brain has been trained for decades to use this as the front line of attack. I have an awareness of this go-to fear response, and it has been a struggle for me to rewire my brain to learn that it is okay and safe when responding to the situation at hand.

The aspect of EMDR that you can incorporate at home is simply going for a walk. The movement of walking, one leg after the next, is a form of bilateral stimulation. The reason this is so helpful is that the emotional discourse that is associated with the main issue of pain is brought to the forefront to work through. Ideally, when a person has processed through the distress of the event, they will have a reduction in triggers. Think back to when I mentioned the soldier coming back from war, feeling deregulated when he/she hears a loud noise. The brain recalls this as gunfire, and the person is likely to experience fear and anxiety. EMDR works to process that fear and regulate the person, so they may hear loud noises, but not have the emotional response anymore.

I can say with credibility, from experience, that EMDR has been a catalyst in this change. I also give credit to Brainspotting, which has helped me to untangle the yarn ball that is the complexity of trauma. Brainspotting works by identifying the spot in the brain where trauma is stuck. In EMDR, a therapist might use alternately vibrating paddles in the client's hands, igniting the bilateral stimulation. In Brainspotting, the therapist will hold a pointer for your eyes to follow as he moves it vertically and horizontally. Then, you identify the point at which it feels most distressing to you. The concept is that this spot is where your unhealed wounds are located, and it opens those emotionally halted places in your brain to be able to work through the memories.

EMDR or Brainspotting is most often used for those with symptoms of mental disorders related to distress, like PTSD or ASD. It is also useful to one who may be struggling with the negative self-beliefs that typically mimic the trauma. Furthermore, these methods assist in making sense of the issues you may be experiencing. It does not mean that there is a particular disorder you have; it means that there is a reason for what you have been facing, and it is worth inspecting. Also, while one type of therapy or technique will help some, it may not prove effective for all. Talk therapy is a favorable tool to access initially, then to continue examining what your needs are moving forward.

Subchapter 4: Counseling

One of my top recommendations is counseling, be it individual, couples, family, etc. This may be in part to the bias I have, being a counselor. Regardless, counseling is relevant and efficient in doing self-work. First and foremost, the base of any therapeutic relationship is safety and trust. Safety and trust are crucial components that are missing in an occurrence of trauma. For a counselor to provide these vital restorative attributes commences the healing journey. Moreover, counseling gives way to start talking about the emotional disturbances one experiences and typically what unhealthy coping behaviors or mental health issues they have. In any typical case, the presenting issue the client presents with is not the true issue at the core; there are trauma and/or attachment issues. With time, and as the layers shed off, one can process through the past. There are several theories of counseling that have proven effectiveness for the treatment of trauma. However, counseling will not be successful if you are not ready to do the work.

It is imperative that your choice to work through your issues is an intrinsic desire, as motivation cannot come solely from an extrinsic reason. In recovery programs, a common saying is that you will lose anything you put before recovery. This applies to your healing from trauma, too, because if you place someone or something else before your own healing, then you will not succeed as fluently. Unhealthy ways of blocking emotions pertaining to trauma will prevent access to remediating these disturbances in a way that is supportive and in first consideration of you.

Subchapter 5: Exercise

Another common method to overcoming trauma is with exercise because it enables one to treat the physical aspect of healing. A useful method to release this trauma is to start noticing how your body feels. It is noticing the depth of breath, the soreness or aches in certain areas, and the tension or tightness of muscles. This is a good way to spot out where trauma may be stored. With this information, you can pay attention to and care for those areas of the body. Once aware of this, you can fuel your body with what it needs.

Many have shared their experience with running or

high-intensity interval training as helpful tools to feeling empowered and reengaged with their bodies. Most who have experienced a complex or lengthy duration of trauma will dissociate, to prevent from further harm. I have known many patients who have said that they have not interacted with their bodies in years. Basically, the body recognizes the potential or actual harm that is being inflicted. As a survival skill, the mind shuts our system down to self-protect from agony. As a reminder, the restoration of your relationship to your body is imperative on this journey.

I suggest you find what works for you—what gives you that sense of being alive again, where you once felt dead. Due to your biological nature, and the ways we were created with built-in protection, our bodies are long-suffering and can endure copious amounts of agony before it is all released. Furthermore, remediating the body coincides with working out the kinks in your head, too. And this is where therapy and touching the unproductive cognitions become exponentially obliging.

Subchapter 6: Grounding Exercises

Grounding exercises help you decrease your anxiety and bring you back to center. The main categories for grounding tools are mental, physical, and soothing. Mental grounding tools may be describing the detail of your environment, counting backwards by 3's, or playing a naming all cities that start with the letter "A". This is another tool you can use to connect to the logical part of your brain to decrease emotional disturbance. Physical grounding techniques are to become aware of your senses. An easy way to use this is to think of what you see, hear, smell, touch, and taste at that moment. A couple of ideas I mentioned earlier, like breathing, yoga, and exercise, also fall into this category. Other options are putting your whole face into a sink of cold water, clenching and releasing your fists, or having a grounding object. A grounding object can be a squishy ball, Play-Doh, or a smooth rock. Lastly, there are soothing techniques utilized for grounding. Examples of soothing techniques are sharing about your favorite season, color or place. Positive self-talk is another way to soothe and ground you. [v]

Additionally, it is important to identify a safe place, whether real or imagined. This could be a favored beach or a spot in the grass under a shade tree. A safe place is beneficial for lessening emotional deregulation. In this safe place, you can imagine a container to place those emotions, memories, or thoughts in to process later. You might also consider having a tangible container to write down what you want to process later. You would put this in the container to compartmentalize the stressor(s) until you are ready to discuss this with someone safe and trusted.

Chapter 4: Understanding Recovery From Trauma

They say we spend much of our adult lives recovering from childhood. While, as daunting and tedious as this statement sounds, it is true. The exception is the way this work on yourself is perceived. You can see it as daunting and tedious or through a lens that displays growth and prosperity of mental and physical health. Though it is not an easy downhill ride with the wind in your hair type of work. It feels more like you are in a triathlon, and in case you did not know this: you are absolutely worth every uphill, strenuous climb and grueling breaststroke.

Subchapter 1: Healing Trauma

In consideration of those deep, expansive waters of the ocean metaphor, it appears to be quite comparable to each individual person. There's the shore. The shore is the shallow, safe place to let others see glimpses of you. Fortunately, the shore does not put your truest self on display-that is to be hidden and kept underneath the dark-blue curtains. At least, that is the message that we are reminded of early on. Especially when those elephant tears are emerging from the emotional abyss. The transparent, rough patch between the shore and the deep- those are the behaviors. It gives away a little more about what is going on under the surface. It shows the way in which we treat ourselves, and as a result, treat the world. A bit farther out, it appears to be safer. There is less commotion from what the eye can see, yet enclosed is that expanse of life history, trauma, hardship, fond memories, emotions, thoughts, you name it- it is there. We tend to care for those fragile pieces of us in a far more delicate fashion. We are quick to move when anyone or anything starts toward those sensitive aspects of us. If you are as human as I am, you know exactly what I am talking about. If we are feeling brave, sometimes we offer another to grab a life jacket and head for the deep-end. Perhaps, this is our bravest day, and we snorkel- the goggle mask, flippers and all. It is in those vulnerable and receptive times that we feel connected and loved.

It is in those times that we heal and grow the most. The question is: Can I conjure up the courage to be more vulnerable and dive deep with a companion?

I supposed I stayed on the shore long enough, and that was not working for me anymore. The ache in my stomach appeared to turn itself inside out, then outside in, on repeat when I entertained the idea of sharing how I felt and what I had gone through. Yet, I held strong to my determination and counted slowly under my breath, noticing any slight aid the oxygen would give my clenched, anxious chest. This feeling was all too recognizable- there was a huge ball of fear, wrapped in the solace of familiarity. I knew I needed to see how my trauma-infected brain could respond in a brand-new way to this idea of being open with someone else. I cannot speak enough about the key component of having a solid community with you to help you along the way. The backbone of working to become healthy is spirituality. Spirituality presents a new strength and power you have over what you were formerly powerless, and it reminds you that you really are not alone in this.

Subchapter 2: Coming Into The Present Moment

The vitality of coming into the present moment makes a catastrophic change in healing from adversities. Again, think of the split between the mind and body when going through hard times. It is natural and quite easy to separate from reality when reality is too harsh and scary to be in. There are some days, where I realize I have not recognized or paid attention to my body the entire day. I have been in my head the whole time and have missed the connection, again. I have found myself on a yoga mat, where I felt totally present with my body, and that evoked anxiety in me. I had not been connected to me, in that way, for so long. It was new to me; it was unfamiliar and frankly terrifying.

Being in the present moment contradicts the dissociation of the mind and body. I often hear people say that it is important to listen to your body and trust it. This is foreign to anyone who has a tough past. My body was violated; my body betrayed me- the list goes on. These statements make it even harder to trust when this is the belief we have held onto for so long. What is necessary for turning this around, is recognizing them as untruths and realizing that you actually can trust yourself and your body. You will be okay. When you can soothe yourself by gently calming your negative self-talk, this begins to change your reactions to this opposition.

My guess is that those paper tigers that is fear hold you hostage to those thoughts and behaviors. So, how is it I can deal with the fear, anger or any bitter emotion that is leading me? Simply, welcome the emotion- let it be present with you. Let yourself be present with the emotion. I recommend you personify the emotions, give them names, configure what they look like, and hold their hand- befriend them. The only way to feel you have control over your emotions is to be in awareness of them and allow them to be in your space. If you do not, they will try to take up more space and more control; at least that is how it feels. Another good idea is to express gratitude to your feelings for serving their purpose. Likely, these emotions and the coping tools you had helped you survive childhood, adolescence or whatever life stage you are in. You get to direct them to take a seat while you make the big decisions. When you pair this with recognizing, acknowledging and breathing deeply, your mind and body become one again.

You always have your breath, so pay attention to it. By being in tune with your breath, it will help to narrow your focus on what is centering and mostly controllable. When you do this, you can begin to slow down each breath. The inhales and exhales remind you to be with yourself, and you can set an intention for how you can offer yourself goodness that day. You may even welcome your inner child to reparent her/him.

As previously discussed, everyone has an inner child; and typically, to find him/her, you look to where your heart aches most. This child is not to be left alone in that dark spot, but to be brought to light and cared for. It is incredible to see how this reconnection with your younger self directs you to what you need to heal from. Since your inner child is often the one driving when you feel alert and out of sorts, you can learn to be gentle with yourself in this process and begin to see that your inner child is not one to fear, but one to re-engage and take seriously. It is not your fault that you did not have healthy relationships, communication or coping modeled for you as a child. You did the best with what you knew. This is the time to protect and unconditionally love your little self. This will help in finding the cords that attach the logical and emotional parts of your brain.

Subchapter 3 Factors & Variables Of Trauma

There is a complicated relationship between the two forces of the brain: the prefrontal cortex and the amygdala. We discussed how these parts work together to create a person's foundational functions.

Yet, they are opposing forces at the same time; logic and reasoning vs. emotion and instinct. At times, it feels like there is a battle going on in my mind; I am trying my very best to help the underdog, my prefrontal cortex, to pull through when the survival instincts from trauma feel generously strong.

I presumed that not everyone had this warfare breaking out in his or her mind. I decided that rather than suspecting what others were going through, I could get help and focus on finding victory. If not victory, at least I could still the waters a little bit. I decided to see a therapist and open up about all that I had been enduring.

When I first began working on my emotional and mental health, it felt easy for me to want to give up on any sort of justification or rationalization. I will share my personal experience with this, as everyone goes through the anxieties around deciding whether to start the work or not. This was one of the first times my good decision-making skills came out victorious in the battle opposing my survival techniques. I was able to gather my thoughts, recognize I needed help and take the initiative like a well-put-together human. At least, that is what I am convincing myself to be these days.

Hesitantly, I trailed my therapist down the hallway, glancing up and down, side to side. It was like I was playing a brief game of detective, observing every marking, each crack, all the intricate details I could lay my eyes on. I noticed the exposed brick that dropped the temperature a good couple degrees as we became encompassed by it. I started to smell an amber/wood musk coming from the door upon which we were entering. A soothing candle burning just ahead- a simple reminder that there is always a touch of light in the darkness. The color that most aesthetically appeases me is a dark teal/navy color, and that seemed to be hers, too. I plopped down on the velvet, beautifully colored couch. As I sank down into the impression my body created, I felt an ease come over me. That knot in my stomach dissipated; the pressure in my chest died down. I was ready.

There had been times when I would gain the courage to open that vice, and outward appeared the formation of gloomy, dark clouds precipitating rain and landing harshly on my skin. My whole body was under the fire of a million little pins and needles impenetrably pattering me. Not only did trauma pierce a hole in me, but it also punctured a hole in my family, my character, and my beliefs of the world and myself. The world I once knew was collapsing in front of my eyes and I felt powerless to make any attempt in changing it. So many of us believe we are imprisoned by devastating events during our lifetime because the impacts of trauma can be shattering to the person who they once understood themselves to be.

As these words fall on to the page, I am reminded of how far I have come since those life-changing events. It has been about 20 years since I started an on-again, off-again, relationship with individual therapy, self-help books, and just about anything I could do to rewire my mind, body, and soul. So, 20 years is a long time, and that is far from a typical case. One could very possibly heal in just a few counseling sessions or a left-field method of healing. Again, the focus of healing is for you to give yourself what you needed and a good way to start that is to find a tool that helps you be there for yourself.

Time and intimacy were extraordinary factors in my journey back to the surface. There is no magic button for healing your past. It is not just one therapy session, and I am good to go. If only it were this easy. Once you have worked through one issue, it usually leads to another. To be honest, it can be frustrating at times. There are moments where I think I am recovered from an incident in the past, all to see that there is another layer of growing to be had. Take heart in knowing that it is cathartic to cry and empowering to do this work for yourself. Once the layers start peeling back, it becomes less cumbersome.

Subchapter 4: Trauma Disorders

It is beneficial to see a physician for flu-like symptoms, as they test you for the flu, and notify you that you tested positive or negative for it. For this example, we will say you tested positive. In an ambivalent way, you are relieved that you know what you are experiencing and can now treat it. The same applies to mental health illnesses and diagnoses. I want to share more about a well-known disorder, PTSD. After hearing about the signs and symptoms of PTSD, it may bring you a sense of relief knowing that you are not the only one out there living with such suffering. While these disorders have numerous similarities of symptoms, there are a few noteworthy differences. The differentiating factor is mostly the duration of time a person has the symptoms. A diagnosis of PTSD may be given if the symptoms persist for over one month. [17]

Symptoms of ASD and PTSD are intrusive symptoms, negative mood, avoidance symptoms, and hyperarousal symptoms. Intrusive symptoms include an array of visual recollections of the traumatic event such as flashbacks, memories, and nightmares. Typically, these evoke the emotional disturbance that makes it appear that a person is re-experiencing the initiating event. A negative mood is categorized by one feeling either the hyper/hypo arousal from the high level of stress. The negative mood may be portrayed through a very low, depressive state of being or a highly reactive and perhaps volatile mood. Often, this is viewed similarly to depression or Bipolar I or II Disorder. [15]

Furthermore, avoidance symptoms can be identified when a person does not revisit the people, places, and things that are reminders of the originating event. This avoidance method is used as a self-protection measure to prevent any trauma from surfacing. Lastly, hyperarousal symptoms are what I had previously noted and can also include: being restless, easily irritated, lacking focus, and feeling flighty or hyperaware and alert. [14]

Hopefully, this is making sense for you out of what has been going on. It is normal to have only been through one or two of these symptoms. Nevertheless, it may still seriously impact you and your functioning. If that is the case, it is worth looking at what you may need to live free of these impairments. Keep in mind that the many levels of treatments and daily tools are available to you, and you can access what is going to fit your circumstances best.

Chapter 5: Learning To Heal

I could no longer remain afloat, my head slowly bobbing for air as each commotion of the wave struck me. As I gradually fell into the infinite subterranean, it felt like a film was cast in my line of sight. The film played my story. It began with my earliest memories. I saw my youngest self, spritely and bright at age four, dashing through the sprinkler with my wet, ragged dog. I watched as my parent's divorce, which initiated my innate longing for a father. I watched as he left our house and moved across town. I saw my older sister becoming my best friend, even after the countless times we fought in those typical sibling brawls. There was the abandonment of a close friend group the day I returned to school after being sick. The day my mother's boyfriend moved in, and my safety moved out. I would spend my afternoons at my grandparent's house, playing with the couple monotonous toys there were and watching some old-timey cartoons. My grandfather would help me with homework, particularly the math that went over my head. I noticed that sitting on his lap, while we worked on math, only reiterated my lack of safety. I could not seem to find a place where I'd have stability and safety. It was there, and I learned that love meant giving my body to others and it is better to be seen than heard.

My identity and self-worth were drowning long before my physical body. The film went on, showing my accomplishments of graduating high school and excelling at sports. In college, I was introduced to friends that were outright no good for helping me reroute the pathways of lie that my trauma history etched so indelibly in my mind. And, boy, I sure needed that. My self-image and esteem plunged. I found myself dating a completely emotionally unavailable young man. This resembled what I knew, so of course, the familiarity drew me. As I am still strolling through this film of my life's timeline, the next chapter was the absolute hardest to witness. I was 18 years of age, and so low on the totem pole of self-love, it was likely a world record. This chapter was the heart-wrenching chapter that premiered my lowest moment- this was the ultimate abandonment of self and the moment I hit the ocean floor.

I refuse to let the story end there. I was undoubtedly starting from square one, even after those eighteen years of life. I was empty, unfulfilled, and tired. I was just tired of being run over by anyone who wanted it his or her way and devalued me. There was nothing to give, and maybe worse, nothing to receive. The tape played on, and it took me hours of counseling, numerous self-help resources, receiving support and love from others and God. I saw myself slowly building, brick by brick, breathe by breath, my new self that was not going to abandon herself. There were plenty of excruciatingly hard days, particularly dealing with the "shore" and "tide" parts of my ocean. It was I, in a place of reckoning with the behaviors, negative self-talk, and addictions. As strenuous as the backsliding was, I kept on. To this day, I am wholly grateful for the work I have done to prove to myself how worthy I am on reclaiming my power, showing up for myself, and living a life full of trust and love.

I imagine myself sitting in the cool, damp sand. It's just before dusk, and the sun is slowly making its way back to warm up the sand. The ocean waves are crashing against the shore, and I am sitting there, so small, so human, so at peace with my trauma. I notice the deep- it is not so frightening anymore. I notice a calmness in its presence- or maybe that is just my own. I am reminded of that shaggy, orange carpet in that musky old therapy lobby. But, this time, it is different. I am not sitting in fear; I am facing those tigers. I'm free from the burdens that once held me down. This time I am not covered in shame from each Big T and little t. I am open to exploring more of the mysterious ocean.

I am a believer that we were made connect to others. It is part of our basic needs as human beings. Someone once told me that the opposite of trauma, pain, and hurt is connection and love. So, I am here to say that if it were not for me seeking out fulfilling and equal relationships, I do not know quite where I would be. Those relationships and my relationship with God made all the difference as I worked through all of it.

Subchapter 1: Paths To Recovery

There is an array of techniques and tools to add to our repertoires, and this is great news because they are available to every one of us. The most important part of placing labels on your life experiences is seeing that you can change how it looks in your future. Intermittently, I have shared ideas and tools for you to utilize and build your restoration capital. The remainder of the book will focus heavily on that, as healing is utterly attainable.

The language we use when we talk to others or ourselves is imperative to tend. We need to speak kindly and lovingly to ourselves, especially if that was not given to us as a child. In a greater sense, this is another piece to unlearning what is not useful and providing what was needed that we did not receive. If you have experienced mental, emotional, intellectual, psychological, or any other type of abuse, it is common for you to take those comments or scrutiny to hear are to believe it to be the truth about you. This is the tricky part of trauma and the shame with which it is paired. My guess is that you have taken on a phrase, like "I am stupid." Or "I am ugly." as part of your self-schema. You believe these things because, at the time, you did not have a filter to know that you did not have to accept other people's criticism as your reality. It is time to reframe what you have previously thought to be true about you, to what is truly accurate. This gentle and reparative language will drive out the forces of shame that hold us hostage to trauma.

Furthermore, a way to counteract these negatives statements is best done with a couple of positive ones. If the phrase is "I am stupid." You would say, "I am smart. I am wise. I have common sense." By saying a statement, a couple of times, it helps the brain to recognize that there is another course it can take when locking in the information, especially when the information is entering more frequently than that of the negative information.

Self-leadership originates here, as you dictate what goes in and goes out of your mind. This gives direction for where you want to guide yourself. Having positive self-talk initiates a natural trait of leadership. This looks like scheduling your days, weeks, and months to be filled with self-care and setting and fulfilling goals. When you set goals that are measurable and tangible, you gain encouragement, knowing that you are doing a lot for yourself and for those around you, too. Goals are achievements you desire for your future, and you must be able to track down your progress toward them by completing the smaller goals, as well as your ultimate goal. In the instance of healing trauma, that cannot simply be a goal, as it is broad and intangible. You can set your goal as: I will participate in counseling one time weekly for four weeks to reduce my anxiety level from a 10 to a 5. By creating short-term goals, you will be encouraged that you are getting somewhere with the effort you are putting into your self-work. A helpful tip is to write this out on a calendar or whiteboard, somewhere you can see it every day. You will be reminded of what you are working toward and be able to note your progress along the way.

So far, we have healthy self-talk and goal setting, as pillars of self-leadership and by setting and maintaining boundaries. A boundary is not a wall, or for that matter, a fortress around you to protect from any risk. A boundary is not to keep you isolated inside without others to comfort you. A boundary also is not allowing others the margin to trample over you. Boundaries are nonexistent when we live in disarray and are not taught early in life when it is important to know how to protect our sense of peace best. Boundaries are a catalyst when it comes to maneuvering through your life. When you have boundaries, you say no to what is not good for you and yes to what is. You get to choose what you do and do not want to do and decide what is and is not acceptable. In this, a new light shines on you, giving yourself what you did not get when you needed it most, and you get to give it to yourself.

Setting boundaries looks like you are protecting your harmony in the capacity of physical, emotional, intellectual, mental, and financial aspects of your life. You know that feeling you get in your gut when something is wrong? That is a pretty good place for you to go to check in about what type of boundary you may need to set. Boundaries are crucial when it comes to trauma in order to prevent trauma repetition. It is natural for us to go to recreate traumatic experiences from before; it is what we learned. Often, we reenact our traumas to replay our past, in turn, hoping to find resolve, but ultimately adding another layer to the original wound.

Subchapter 2: Creating Structure

The term structure is defined as a support system that is organized and provides stability. Note the contrast here to what home was like growing up. When trauma is present, you can always count on chaos, instability, and mistrust being there, too. Structure is essential to reestablishing your foundation and recreating your life.

In the day-to-day, it will be important to have a routine set. It can be that you work from 8a.m. to 4p.m. each day, and you have time either before or after work to exercise and spend the rest of your day with a friend, a book, or a bubble bath. It is what works for you, but it is crucial you manage your time well and provide yourself with structure. It helps me to plan out my week on a couple of different platforms; I will schedule out my personal and professional calendars, along with my whiteboard calendar at my house. I use different colors to identify where my time is going. I value relationships, so I spend a lot of time growing them. On the other hand, I can let my budgeting or passive incomes fall by the wayside, which does not afford me with steadiness. Being cognizant of where my time is going, will establish a quality of life that I am wanting; not one that I am dreading and of which

I feel out of control. There are times when I am unbalanced in the time I put into different values. If I greatly value time spent with my friends and family, but I am depositing most of my waking hours into work, then I can maneuver my schedule to arrange for more gatherings with friends and family. If I highly value and prioritize relationships and exercise, but lack in growing professional and financially, I can figure out how to honor my values, while moderating the other facets. Balance is an aspect of your value system that you can examine weekly or monthly, and you will find where there are incongruences and how to shift your priorities.

Subchapter 3: Self-Care

Self-care will be your confidant in the course of moving through difficult times. When you are emotionally and physically drained from processing through trauma, it is imperative you pay service to your wellbeing. Self-care looks like, speaking kindly to yourself, giving yourself grace and time, eating healthy and drinking plenty of water, and bettering your financial health by budgeting regularly. It is spending time with friends and family who are life-giving and guide you where you want to go. It is also continuing to learn about you, others, interesting subjects, and new activities. Ultimately, self-care and structure work together to assist with your self-leadership. There is a multitude of ideas on how this can look and what types of self-preservation/protection you may want to consider.

Think of the latest time you "OK'd" spending money on yourself to go out for a nice dinner or taking an hour out of your day to relax in the sun with a book. Consider what it meant when you paused to center yourself by journaling and praying. With the hustle and bustle of society, the self is usually the first forgotten. By no means does spending money on you have to be a costly endeavor. Simply, it is doing something, or not doing something, to obtain a state of joy. This is also where choosing yourself becomes paramount, which is not to be looked at in a selfish way. Decide what it is you need to feel secure and content and do that thing. Again, it's you not accepting what is not good for you or saying "no" to a request that already feels overwhelming. Some of you may see this as an everyday task you already do, and others may see this as frightening. Here are ways you can go about this.

Look for a counselor. You may search for specifics for whom you are searching, i.e., a female counselor who specializes in trauma work and is certified in EMDR. Plan to get your body moving. This does not have to be a drastic shift from your normal day-to-day routine. If you have not run since the Summer after high school, mark your calendar for 30-minute walks for 3-days a week. Search for some yoga classes—if finances are holding you back, check for free or donation-based classes. Download a free meditation app. Five minutes a day takes up just a small moment in your date. These few minutes can make a world of difference. Particularly, it helps to slow breathing, lessen anxiety and live more presently. Follow through on caring for yourself. This is you making an investment for your future because you deserve to live a happy, healthy life.

Chapter 6: The Silver Lining Of Trauma

There is no stress-free way out of trauma; you have to go through it, not around, over, or under it. You did not walk one mile into the forest to get out in two quick steps. You did not find your way in the middle of the ocean only to get to the shore with two butterfly strokes. When working through your past, by way of counseling, group therapy, etc. the term "we" is vital. You are not alone in dealing with your suffering, but you cannot put the responsibility on someone else to do it for you. You are accountable for your emotional healing and your response to trauma. You may not have had the power to choose what happens or what does not happen, but you get to choose how you deal with it moving forward. This is the vigor of working with others, and the control you get back what was lost from this trauma.

Choose a positive community that will leave you fulfilled and be there when you need them. Choose to care for your body by feeding it well and moving it. Decide to seek a higher power, to believe in something greater than yourself and your trauma. Elect to love yourself, again, or for the first time. You have what you need to do, so do it. It is up to you to set guidelines with those who are not optimistically influencing your life. You can choose not to partake in relationships that are damaging to any part of you. It is up to you, no one else, to put in the work to practice new coping tools, rewrite your story and change the way you view yourself and the world around you. You get to be worry-free going out into the deep.

Subchapter 1: How To Develop A Support Network

It is natural to feel lonely when you have been alone in trying to keep your head above water from all the burdens you carry. It is almost blinding, to be honest. Being able to see that there is a community surrounding you seems non-existent in the face of trauma. One of the first and likely hardest steps is to reach out for support. It may be a disease of the ego or pride, but it is difficult to let someone else know that we are in need of connection and belonging. This is our innate desire as humans; I consider the need for a community to be a basic need.

Here are some ideas on how to get used to the idea that you will need others around you during this process. We will start in some small ways, so it is not overwhelming. You can start by looking at community support groups, group counseling, or therapy online. The notion that you are open and interested in this may evoke some anxiety, but it also could be a start for you to see that you do need help. Spiritually asking for help is another way to start by asking for help. You can journal to be able to feel some relief from carrying the trauma. However, the idea of being with someone and being able to work through your hardships is the main point.

If you feel comfortable with asking others to support

you, then the next step is finding those people. You may already have family or friends who you find to be your confidants. You do not have to let them know all that you are going through, but you can be honest about some of your struggles. Contrary to what the trauma in our mind tells us that we will be looked down up or less than, we will be seen as strong for being able to share about our hard times. More often than not, the person or persons we tell will have gone through or are currently going through similar issues.

Willingly, the feelings of being alone in the world slip away. You may feel a bit of an emotional hangover from your vulnerability, but what matters more is that you feel the relief from getting it off your chest. Keep in mind that a safe person is one who will treat you with loving-kindness in response to what you let them in on. This person will not compile shame or guilt on you, but rather respond in a caring manner. If one does not meet you in this way or with empathy, they may not be the best person to reach out to for support.

It is great to have a solid support system, and how to find and build one can be the hardest part. When seeking out support, pay attention to what your intuition tells you or base this on what references you retrieve from others. Ask yourself: Do I feel comfortable and safe with this person? Have they shown me they are loyal and dependable? Do I find them to be trustworthy? How do they treat me? How do I treat myself after being with them? When you can ask yourself these questions and all of the answers come out to be healthy and good for you, then you can count this person to your social support bank.

Someone once told me that replaying or reliving trauma is related to how we treat ourselves. If I continue to dismiss my needs based on how others treat me or how I treat myself, then I will find myself in a pattern of trauma. Furthermore, I will not be able to heal when I am activating my trauma continually fully. Therein lies the concept that when you choose what will serve you best, not in a selfish manner, but in a self-care manner, then you will be working to heal yourself of trauma. I suggest revisiting the subchapter on boundaries or reading more on the subject. This will help you to understand and establish self-care and leadership.

Subchapter 2: Learning To See & Embrace Our "Selves"

I can see myself in a mirror, in the reflection of a window or in a shadow on the concrete. In the visual sense of "seeing myself", I can easily do that. There is a stark contrast to actually seeing myself, in the sense that I can see myself for all I am, any more yet, come to accept and love myself for it. As I mentioned in the introduction, this is not a walk in the park. It comes each time, as times moves forward.

The first time I really saw myself, I cannot remember so well. I do remember myself at different ages are the pictures I have of them in my head. I think of little me as a bright, sociable girl, who as she grew older in childhood, became angry and shy. I noticed her growing old to become a popular yet dramatic and emotionally unstable girl. I see her at eighteen, with her face cast downward and her body feeble. I see her in her mid-twenties rising up to be a strong woman, who is standing up for all the younger selves that she sees within. This is what healing looks like, and this is what is available to you as you continue to choose yourself and well-being each day.

It is one thing to "see" myself; it is another thing to embrace myself. To me, embracing myself looks like this concept of standing up for myself. It is a peculiar perspective to take when what I have known is the opposite. It has been a matter of me letting others treat me like a doormat and not being able to stand up for myself. Boundaries are sometimes troubling when I set them and even more so when I attempt to maintain them. I sometimes feel guilty when I say "no" to someone or lose their approval. When in fact, I am only responsible for my needs, feelings, and responses; I am not responsible for the needs, feelings, and responses of others. All of these ways, I have gone about my life have been externally motivated and based on validation from the world.

The reality I uncovered was that I need to be intrinsically driven and affirmed in order to embrace myself. Some situations and relationships make it a lot easier to do so, and others are a lot tougher. Regardless, when I am confident in who I am and have been able to validate myself, good and bad, I am far less shaken by the opinions and requests of others. I can say "no" to the asks that do not do me well, and I can filter through what others say to me. This filter is crucial to have, as I let the good in and keep the bad out. I do not have to take on the statements, views or beliefs of others. I am grounded and solid in my own beliefs since I have embraced who I am.

Chapter 7: The Stages Of Forgiveness

Someone once told me that forgiveness is for the giver; that was an "aha moment" for me. I used to perceive forgiveness as it was the other person's responsibility to apologize for their actions, then I could forgive them. It was not anything I could do to find that forgiveness. The number one reason that it did not and does not work is that that would be something outside of myself that I am attempting to change, and do not have control or power over. It was when she said that to me that I recognized that forgiveness is for me to find restoration. I had to forgive others, and myself, to be freed from that bondage.

There are common myths that people believe to be accurate of forgiveness. The mere falsities evoke confusion and make us question what we are doing when we consider forgiving someone. There are questions of whether you are giving someone a free pass on the harm they inflicted upon you or perhaps, you have just brushed it aside, minimizing how it affected you. That would be repressing the incident or burying it further down with the others. Instead, forgiveness is to be brought to the surface and rummaged through, to find a way out of being bogged down by carrying the resentment. By defining forgiveness, you can see what it is and remove any other notion that you may have thought to be right before. That is if it is not helpful and actually is not correct.

Forgiveness is a minute-by-minute, hour-by-hour, day-by-day kind of action. When I learned of forgiveness, I was really hoping that it was a one-and-done type of deal. Unfortunately, that is merely not the case. I had the choice to mark the initial notion of forgiveness toward others or myself. On the days it is really hard to do, I get to continue choosing forgiveness until I feel reconciled. I figured if I do not forgive others or myself, it does not make my life worth the while. We will examine the stages of forgiveness together; this will be a good judge of where you are at in the process with certain situations. The stages are not linear, and most of the time there appears to be no rhyme or reason for the cyclicality of forgiveness.

Forgiveness is seen in a variety of ways and the process in which to go about it. I will describe to you the steps that I deem necessary to walk through. These steps are not in a linear order, nor are they steps you complete and check off the list. Visualize the ascending shape of a tornado or a strand of DNA; this is representative of the rungs of forgiveness and grief. The bottom point of the spiral represents the pit of resentment and anger. The starting point of forgiving and grieving precedes the point of pre-contemplating that either of these actions is available to you. Normally, anger and resentment keep us in the dark, unable to see that there is a different way to live. Wherever it is that you gain the concept of this way of modifying, you move into the next steps of forgiveness. At the point, you start to absolve some of that seemingly binding bitterness. This is also the active initiating point of grieving, as grief is an ordinarily forgotten aspect of forgiveness. Even when the person you make amends with appears not to be a particular part of your life anymore, you will still grieve the loss of them. This is purely a fragment to the art of forgiveness. Once you deem it necessary to shift your form of rationale to being open-minded about this life alter, you will inch your way up the ladder, one rung at a time. The circulating of the cyclonic figure or the twists of the DNA strand depict that forgiveness will not be an easy climb, but rather one that has setbacks and stumbles. After a few steps in reverse, then you move onward even farther. This back and forth motion can be a game of Tug-of-War where you meet yourself with resistance or you embrace and accept that this is just the game of life.

Subchapter 1: Stage 1 Of Forgiveness

Lead by becoming aware of what circumstance occurred that you are resentful about, and consider whom you get to forgive. Take note of the basic emotions that emerge: angry, sad, happy, and mad.

Check-in with yourself on what you are feeling that is connected to the person you want to forgive. Let us look at anger at being the emotion that you identified. Anger is known to be a secondary emotion that masks resentment, pain, fear, shame or another that you want to resist experiencing. This is the indicator that will direct you to the start of this process. Write down the name of the person and the event(s). Keep in mind that each part of this is healing, so writing down the name and event may be something you have yet to do. Once you see it on paper, you can write down who and what you forgive. Then, you can speak it aloud and continue to be engaged in how you are feeling.

It is key to be very specific here, as you are dealing with that particular person and situation and that memory is stuck in your neural network. It will be less effective to say, and I forgive my mother for the mean comments she has said to me. You could say I forgive my mom for saying that I am not that great of a person. You may find there are several comments within the broad topic of "mean comments", so write down all that you can think of that needs to be forgiven.

Once you give acknowledgment to what has hurt you, and who has hurt you, you can recognize the differentiation between the action and the actual person. They are not bad people, but they did a bad thing. You can write down characteristics that are negative and positive of this person, to see them for who they are as a whole. This helps you to recognize that there is a high chance this person acted the way they did toward you because they, themselves, were hurting. You have heard the phrase hurt people, hurt people. This helps you to become a little more detached, in a healthy way, from this unforgiveness. Then, you get to move toward the next step of forgiveness.

Subchapter 2: Stage 2 Of Forgiveness

Bring the original emotion you identified to mind and let yourself just be with it. This is a challenge, as it has been easier to ignore and/or avoid the emotions pertaining to what you are attempting to block out or forgive. It is tremendously helpful to create an entity for the emotion- with a name, figure, color, etc. This way, it is somewhat separated from you in a way where you can access your logic better. The act of separating from your emotions to recognize and accept them provides you with more healing room.

Perhaps you have a conversation with this emotion and take ownership of the emotions. Though we may have had terrible things happen to us, we are still responsible for how we respond to it. We are also responsible for choosing to unpack the emotional baggage or carry it with us every day. So, deal with the emotions, do not run from them anymore. Inevitably, they will come up, so it is wise to undergo the process of dealing with them than it is to keep them suppressed.

You may have the thoughts that you learned early on

in life, about showing emotion or crying is being weak, which is truly not the case. Crying is a way to release emotion and experience catharsis. It helps you to acknowledge your pain, knowing it is valid, and you are still okay, working through emotions will not harm you. Some may prefer to be alone while doing this or with a counselor, friend or someone else with whom they feel safe. Whatever you need during this process, remind yourself that you are not alone in it and everyone experiences a level of grief and resentment in working through forgiveness.

Subchapter 3: Stage 3 Of Forgiveness

As we make changes, we tend to have old patterns of thinking arise. These thought patterns are probably cognitive distortions, like justification, catastrophizing, or denying, for example. Justification may look like you trying to provide yourself or someone else with reasons as to why you should not forgive yourself or the other person. Minimization is another distorted cognition that leads to you deciding that what you or the other person did does not amount to needing forgiveness and then you can decide to let it slide. Catastrophizing the negative event or all of what the person did may shift your mind to thinking it was far worse than what actually happened. You must be careful of the stories you tell yourself, as the story may be embellished as worse than reality. Denying that you get to forgive ties into all of this, as that is, they are that yields the most attention for forgiveness. Denial will keep you blind to what is to be forgiven in order to find freedom from the pains of the past.

As you know full well, the mind is an intricately, powerful tool. The mind can play tricks on use to deceive the amount of control we actually have over our thinking than we believe. More often than not, the mind seems to twist our circumstances and pain into the worst possible way of feeling. Another tool of healing is to take recognition that you have the strength and determination to change these destructive patterns of thinking.

Subchapter 4: Stage 4 Of Forgiveness

Choose to forgive. You can see the situation, the person, and the emotions that are associated; however, seeing them alone will not help you to move through them. You have the choice of whether you want to forgive or not. Forgiveness is an innate response to our troubles. I can let the heartache and sorrow dictate how I am going to move forward, or I can decide to let go and continue doing so each time I feel the need to.

You may find yourself trying to control the situation or deflect by seeking distractions but continue to get back to the space where you can let go of what is bothering you. It is natural to feel like you have not forgiven, after the first time you do it. Your mind is trying to comprehend this new way of thinking, feeling, and living. That is okay. You can continue to forgive again and keep on doing so as much as you need to.

Subchapter 5: Stage 5 Of Forgiveness

Give yourself grace and patience during the process of forgiveness, especially when it comes to forgiving you and being able to perceive your experiences in a new light. This new way of living each day comes when you get to see that the false responsibilities you held and tease through what was someone else's pain that you carried. When you can do this, it is clear to see what you have left to do is forgive yourself and allow yourself to be forgiven. If you are spiritual, you will see that forgiveness, grace, and patience are available to you, and you can decide to live in this light, rather than remaining in the darkness of unforgiveness.

True freedom can and will be experienced in this place; you are not the exception. Some may believe that they are eternally bound to their past, but forgiveness counters this argument with the assurance that it is available to each person who chooses to live in this space. Again, the power of choice becomes your strength and courage to keep driving forward, even when it feels easier to give up.

Conclusion

So, there we have it. There is the skinny on what trauma is and where it comes from. There are cycles, patterns, and generational influences. One point I want to reiterate is that trauma is our response to the event; it is not the event itself. Hence, this is why certain people react more negatively and others, almost nonchalantly. Therein lies the control and power we get to regain from our traumatic experiences. We overviewed various day-to-day tools and techniques for healing trauma. These tools are readily usable to try out to see what you find helpful. Again, what works for some, may not work for others and vice versa.

When we find ourselves in a life-threatening and potentially harmful situation, our brain knows what to do. The purpose of our fear centers is to protect us from harm. The fear responses kick in, whether it is fight, flight, or freeze, and off to the races we go. Initially, this is made to be a very helpful tactic for preventing harm, but when it goes haywire due to continuously being used, that is another story. Trauma becomes lodged in the body, and the brain begins to recognize the triggers that set off that fear response. The midbrain houses both trauma, fear, and other emotions. Thus, with this perfect storm, all bets are off when it comes to trying to maintain composure and emotional sobriety.

Healing from trauma is of the utmost importance. You get to heal from trauma- you do not have to carry it like a 50-lb knapsack all your life. This, my friends, is an enriching truth. So, go the length it takes in therapy, meditate on the good and what serves you and exercise every day. There is that saying, "No one ever said it would be easy; they just said it would be worth it." If they were not talking about healing from emotional wreckage, I am not sure what else would be more applicable.

Moreover, we shored up the big picture of what life

beyond trauma can be, and it is redemptive. You are able to move forward without the baggage of trauma tagging along with you. All in all, your perception creates your reality. You get to decide how you look at trauma and how you choose differently in how you live every day, to change your projected future. Having the control of deciding what each day moving forward looks like, is enough motivation for you to see that the past is not with you anymore. You decide how your future looks.

Ultimately, what I hope you remember is that it is your responsibility to recover from trauma, hardship, loss, etc. No, it may not be fair that you are left with repercussions from this event or these events. Yet, this is the place you get to take back the power you lost in this process. You get to take the high road and choose to heal. You get to consider the idea of what it might be like if you opened yourself up to believe you are enough, worth it and deserve unconditional love. Likely, these thoughts are completely foreign to you. They may have never been spoken to you, or you may have never considered them to be the truth about you. Open yourself to the idea of this and what it might be like if you agree that this is true to who you are. You'll find yourself waiting on the shore, unafraid of the dark, expansive waters you face. You'll see that it was not so scary to let them into that place. You'll notice that petrified feeling, the pit in the core of your stomach, and your shame amounts to nowhere near what it was the first time you saw the ocean. This is the kind of healing you get to have when you brave the deep blue.

References

1. Magner, E. (2018, December 18). What does it actually mean to have a dissociative episode? Retrieved July 14, 2019, fromhttps://www.wellandgood.com/good-advice/what-does-dissociation-feel-like/

2. Ross, C., and Halpern, N. (2009). Trauma Model Therapy: A Treatment Approach for Trauma, Dissociation and Complex Comorbidity. Richardson, Texas: Manitou Communications.

3. Schmidt, N. B., Richey, J. A., Zvolensky, M. J., & Maner, J. K. (2008). Exploring human freeze responses to a threat stressor. Journal of behavior therapy and experimental psychiatry, 39(3), 292–304. doi:10.1016/j.jbtep.2007.08.002

4. Seltzer, L. F., Ph.D. (2015). Trauma and the Freeze Response: Good, Bad, or Both? Psychology Today. Retrieved August 2, 2019, from https://www.psychologytoday.com/us/blog/evolu

tion-the-self/201507/trauma-and-the-freeze-response-good-bad-or-both.

5. Ananda B. Amstadter & Laura L. Vernon (2008) Emotional Reactions During and After Trauma: A Comparison of Trauma Types, Journal of Aggression, Maltreatment & Trauma, 16:4, 391-408, DOI: 10.1080/10926770801926492

6. Befriending Your Body: How Yoga Helps Heal Trauma. (2019, July 15). Retrieved August 2, 2019, from https://kripalu.org/resources/befriending-your-body-how-yoga-helps-heal-trauma

7. Hosier, D. (2019, July 15). Fight, Flight, Freeze or Fawn? Trauma Responses. Retrieved from https://childhoodtraumarecovery.com/all-articles/trauma-responses-fight-flight-freeze-or-fawn/.

8. Staggs, S. (2014). The Big Deal With "Little-t traumas". Psych Central. Retrieved on July 14,

2019, from https://blogs.psychcentral.com/after-trauma/2014/02/the-big-deal-with-little-t-traumas/

9. Steinberg, M., and Schnall M. (2001). The Stranger in the Mirror. New York, New York: Harper.

10. van der Kolk BA. The compulsion to repeat the trauma: re-enactment, revictimization, and masochism. Psychiatr Clin North Am 1989;12(2):389-411.

11. West, M.A. (2016). The psychology of meditation: Research and practice. Oxford, United Kingdom: Oxford University Press.

12. What is EMDR? (n.d.). Retrieved from https://www.emdr.com/what-is-emdr/

13. Steil, R., Dittmann, C., Müller-Engelmann, M., Dyer, A., Maasch, A. M., & Priebe, K. (2018). Dialectical behaviour therapy for posttraumatic

stress disorder related to childhood sexual abuse: a pilot study in an outpatient treatment setting. European journal of psychotraumatology, 9(1), 1423832. doi:10.1080/20008198.2018.1423832

14. (2019, May 12). The mind-based causes of M.E. Retrieved from https://minddetoxtunbridgewells.wordpress.com/2019/05/12/the-mind-based-causes-of-m-e/

15. Najavits, L. M. (2003). Seeking safety: a treatment manual for Ptsd and substance abuse. New York, NY, etc.: The Guilford Press.

16. Iribarren, J., Prolo, P., Neagos, N., & Chiappelli, F. (2005). Post-Traumatic Stress Disorder: Evidence-Based Research for the Third Millennium. Evidence-Based Complementary and Alternative Medicine, 2(4), 503–512. doi: 10.1093/ecam/neh127

17. Nowak, L. (2019, July 16). Acute Stress Disorder vs. PTSD: How They Differ, and Why It Matters. Retrieved fromhttps://www.bridgestorecovery.com/blog/acute-stress-disorder-vs-ptsd-how-they-differ-and-why-it-matters/

18. What Is The Difference Between A Level 1, Level 2, And Level 3 Trauma Center? (2018, December 09). Retrieved August 17, 2019, from https://hospitalmedicaldirector.com/what-is-the-difference-between-a-level-1-level-2-and-level-3-trauma-center/

Disclaimer

The information contained in this book and its components, is meant to serve as a comprehensive collection of strategies that the author of this book has done research about. Summaries, strategies, tips and tricks are only recommendations by the author, and reading this book will not guarantee that one's results will exactly mirror the author's results.

The author of this book has made all reasonable efforts to provide current and accurate information for the readers of this book. The author and its associates will not be held liable for any unintentional errors or omissions that may be found.

The material in the book may include information by third-parties. Third-party materials comprise of opinions expressed by their owners. As such, the author of this book does not assume responsibility or liability for any third-party material or opinions.

The publication of third-party material does not constitute the author's guarantee of any information, products, services, or opinions contained within third-party material. Use of third-party material does not guarantee that your results will mirror our results. Publication of such third-party material is simply a recommendation and expression of the author's own opinion of that material.

Whether because of the progression of the Internet, or the unforeseen changes in company policy and editorial submission guidelines, what is stated as fact at the time of this writing may become outdated or inapplicable later.

written expressed and signed permission from the author.

Lightning Source UK Ltd.
Milton Keynes UK
UKHW011826030220
358089UK00001B/123